John MacArthur

John MacArthur

An Insider's Tribute

Don Green

John MacArthur: An Insider's Tribute
Don Green

Copyright © 2022 Donald Green

ISBN 978-0-9987156-0-5

Cover design and typeset by www.greatwriting.org

Trust the Word Press
575 Chamber Drive
Milford, OH 45150

www.ttwpress.com

TRUST THE WORD
PRESS

To the Board of Directors of Grace to You

whose humble service and skillful leadership have been quietly indispensable to the worldwide spread of the Bible teaching of John MacArthur.

Acknowledgments

Two men are primarily responsible for the artistic beauty found in the pages of this book. The photos of John MacArthur were all taken by Will Moneymaker at various times and locations. Will is not only a brilliant photographer. He is a faithful friend and indispensable partner in every aspect of my ministry. I thank God for him.

The layout and other graphics of the book come to you through the skilled hands of Jim Holmes. His creative brilliance repeatedly amazed me and expanded the possibilities of this book far beyond anything I could have imagined.

This book would not be in your hands apart from Peter Coeler. His counsel and encouragement convinced me to move forward with the project and shaped the entire manner in which I approached the opportunity.

For fifteen years I served on the staff of Grace to You. I have the fondest of memories of our time together and formed lifelong friendships that will continue in heaven. They have my deepest love and respect.

I am grateful to Phil Johnson for writing the foreword to this book. Phil, as most people know, has worked alongside John MacArthur for nearly 40 years. Publicly, he is a warrior for truth. Privately, I have known him as a self-effacing leader and a humble, humorous friend—a true gift from God to me.

It seems superfluous to mention John MacArthur here, since the entire book is a tribute to him. But I specifically want to thank him for making room in his life and ministry for me. No doubt others could have served him better than I did. But God gave the privilege to me for a period of time, and my gratitude is too deep for words.

Of course, my dear wife, Nancy, has walked with me through the times this book describes. She shares the memories described in this book and made valuable contributions to its final form.

The highest and truest honor goes to Christ alone. For all the human love I've mentioned, the love of Christ is supreme. He alone "loved me and gave Himself up for me" (Gal. 2:20). Ultimately, it's to His glory that I send this book to you.

Foreword

This is a sweet personal tribute to John MacArthur, whose biblical teaching and pastoral gifts have blessed multiple generations of believers worldwide. Don Green studied, served, and thrived under John's ministry at Grace Church for more than fifteen years, and he has compiled this scrapbook of anecdotes and recollections about various lessons he learned, and bits of wisdom he absorbed under John's influence.

I, too, have been privileged to have John as my pastor over the past four decades, so my affection for him and my esteem for his giftedness resonate with everything Don Green has written. Reading through Don's observations prompted me to give thanks (as I do daily) for how wonderfully blessed I have been to spend the majority of my life at Grace Church under John MacArthur's pastoral care.

People who know John only from his books and radio ministry often ask me what he is like "in real life." My answer always has been that John is precisely the same in person as he is in the pulpit—full of wise insights, clear-headed, decisive, eager to teach, and easy to learn from. He is also sober-minded but never stuffy; firm in his opinions but not overbearing; and occupied almost completely with biblical and spiritual truth, not trivialities. (We don't generally talk about sports and entertainment over lunch; but about Scripture, the church, and other things of eternal importance.) John's character is defined by kindheartedness, compassion, amiability, and unusual generosity. He is a consistent model of steadfast, immovable integrity, always abounding in the work of the Lord.

Don Green captures all of that and more with these insider's vignettes about things he learned from John MacArthur during his years of ministry at Grace Community Church. Enjoy.

Phil Johnson

Executive Director

Grace to You

Preface

I feel the need to justify the title of this book. It seems brash to call myself an "insider" to John MacArthur and his ministry. For my own sake, if not for yours, I want to clarify what I do and do not mean by the term.

I do not claim to be the *ultimate* insider. I am not John's best friend, most trusted confidante, personal adviser, or golf partner. I never have been. I do not speak with him on a regular basis at this point in my life. Other men fulfill those roles—and do so far better than I could. I would not want to bear false witness by claiming too much.

At the same time, I would be bearing false witness if I didn't acknowledge that I *do* have an insider's perspective on John. I was on the staff of Grace to You from 1996–2012. At first I answered correspondence on his behalf. At the end, I was responsible to oversee the daily operations of the entire ministry. From 2001–2012, my office was immediately next to his. We shared countless conversations and meetings. That gives you some perspective.

Beyond that was my role at Grace Community Church. John first asked me to serve as an elder, and I did so from 2004–2012. During most of that time, I sat immediately to John's left during the monthly elder meetings, as he led us in matters of doctrine and church life. That gives you some additional perspective.

Over the years, John invited me to fill his pulpit and I have had him fill mine. I have interviewed him in public. I have travelled with him. I have been in his home. I have visited him in the hospital. We have countless mutual friends and acquaintances. I now serve on the Grace to You Board of Directors.

With that background, I trust that you won't mind that I use the term "insider" for the purposes of this book. I have seen this prominent pastor in a way that has not been given to most. I emphasize that in part to give you confidence as you read this book. I write from direct, firsthand experience that few, if any, of his faultfinders have.

A sad aspect of long-term spiritual leadership is that "friends" abandon you along the way. It's poignant that, at the end of his apostolic ministry, the apostle Paul would write, "Only Luke is with me" (2 Tim. 4:11) and "At my first defense no one supported me, but all deserted me" (v. 16). It's no secret that men whom John has loved and helped in ministry have recently stood apart from him in some of the battles John has faced. This book is my way of saying, "Not me."

I have known John MacArthur and served alongside him for twenty-five years. He still holds my love and commands my respect—in his various roles as a Bible teacher, pastor, leader, man, and friend. I'm grateful to God that John is alive to see me say it in print.

So I invite you to these pages to see the man that I have seen. You will be encouraged and edified. But what I really hope is that you'll be drawn to the Lord Jesus Christ, who has done such a great work in and through the friend whom I view with esteem and affection.

Remember those who led you, who spoke the word of God to you;
and considering the result of their conduct, imitate their faith.

Hebrews 13:7

Soli Deo Gloria

The Friend of the Bible

For over fifty years, the name of John MacArthur has been virtually synonymous with biblical authority. That's a matter of public record.

What the public has less opportunity to observe is that the life of John MacArthur adorns the doctrine he teaches (*cf.* Titus 2:10). I write this book to supplement the public record so that he might be somewhat better known.

The official, short-form biography of John MacArthur at www.gty.org reads as follows:

> John MacArthur is the pastor-teacher of Grace Community Church in Sun Valley, California, chancellor of The Master's University and Seminary, and featured teacher with the Grace to You media ministry. Grace to You radio, video, audio, print, and website resources reach millions worldwide each day. In more than five decades of ministry, John has written dozens of best-selling books, including *The MacArthur Study Bible, The Gospel According to Jesus, The MacArthur New Testament Commentary* (thirty-four volumes), and *Slave.* He and his wife, Patricia, have four married children and fifteen grandchildren.

That bio, while accurate, doesn't begin to tell the story about John MacArthur, the man. (It also doesn't mention the growing circle of great-grandchildren!) In the pages that follow, I want to add some texture to the picture of a man whose teaching has led so many to a saving and sanctifying knowledge of Jesus Christ.

As you read, you will not find me assigning any sinless perfection to John. His own theology would rebuke me if I tried. John would be the first to say, "By the grace of God I am what I am" (1 Cor. 15:10).

This book is simply a window to see something of that work of God's grace in John's life and ministry.

Nothing more. Nothing less.

For a full-length biography, I highly recommend Iain Murray's book, *John MacArthur: Servant of the Word and Flock* (Banner of Truth, 2011).

The Man Writes Good Books

I was first introduced to the ministry of John MacArthur in 1984. I had been a Christian for less than six months and was wrestling with the issues of the charismatic movement.

A friend recommended John's book *The Charismatics* (Zondervan, 1978) to me. It was the precursor to the better-known *Charismatic Chaos* (Zondervan, 1992). It was among the first ten Christian books I ever purchased.

It was by far the most strategic.

At that formative crossroads in my spiritual life, I read words that changed my spiritual trajectory: "Experience is not the test of biblical truth; biblical truth stands in final judgment on experience" (p. 14).

I immediately thought, "Of course. It could be no other way."

God is God. The Bible is His Word.

That gives Scripture the controlling position in assessing truth claims.

The Bible is the final authority—not the opinions or experiences of man. If your experience contradicts the Bible, your experience is false, no matter how sincere your feelings are about it.

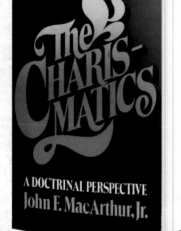

I never struggled with the assertions of the charismatic movement again. In that simple sentence from 1978, John MacArthur gave an anchor to my soul and an aspiration to my heart that has defined my imperfect life and ministry ever since.

The Bible is true. The Bible is precious. The Bible must be taught. The Bible must be defended.

John MacArthur has been doing that for over sixty years.

Pastors like me stand on his shoulders and follow in his wake.

The Bible and only the Bible, to the glory of God alone.

Different By Design
MacArthur
CHARISMATIC CHAOS
MacArthur
Why Government Can't Save You
RIGHT THINKING IN A WORLD GONE WRONG
MACARTHUR
Terrorism, Jihad, and the Bible
John MacArthur
A TALE of TWO SONS
MacArthur
THE HEART of the BIBLE
JOHN MACARTHUR
THE GOD WHO LOVES
JOHN MACARTHUR
KINGDOM LIFE
Matthew 5:1-12
John MacArthur, Jr.
FIRST LOVE
MACARTHUR
STRENGTH FOR TODAY
MACARTHUR
DRAWING NEAR
MACARTHUR
THE FULFILLED FAMILY
JOHN MACARTHUR
STRANGE FIRE
JOHN MACARTHUR
THE TRUTH WAR
JOHN MACARTHUR
Reckless Faith
MacArthur
TWELVE EXTRAORDINARY WOMEN
MACARTHUR
ASHAMED OF THE GOSPEL
MACARTHUR
SHEPHERDOLOGY
THE LOVE OF GOD
John MacArthur, Jr.
THE FREEDOM AND POWER OF FORGIVENESS
MACARTHUR
The Battle for the Beginning
JOHN MACARTHUR
THE GOSPEL ACCORDING TO JESUS
MATTHEW 1-7
MATTHEW 8-15
MATTHEW 16-23
MATTHEW 24-28
MOODY
MACARTHUR
BECAUSE THE TIME IS NEAR
FOLLOW ME
John MacArthur
THE GOSPEL ACCORDING TO PAUL
JOHN MACARTHUR
HARD TO BELIEVE
JOHN MACARTHUR
slave
MACARTHUR
The Power of Suffering
MacArthur
THE QUEST FOR CHARACTER
JOHN MACARTHUR
EXPOSITORY PREACHING
JOHN MACARTHUR, JR.

The Man on the Radio

Yes, I had benefitted from John MacArthur's written ministry in 1984. But as a young man, I still had a lot to learn.

I was still unmarried in 1986. One night I was listening to a Christian station on my car radio. Someone I had not heard before was teaching the Bible. I was drawn to the teaching out of 1 Corinthians 13—the great love chapter in Scripture.

I agreed with the speaker until he said, "If you don't have love, you are nothing. Zero. You don't even matter."

I reacted against that. Truth be told, it hit too close to home to my selfish heart. I pulled my car into the driveway and made a simple but consequential decision.

I had to listen to the end so that I could identify this speaker. I had to protect myself from his dogmatic teaching. If I knew his name, I could turn away from his teaching and protect my spiritual life forever.

I sat in the driveway until the bitter end.

You know how this story ends, right?

"You've been listening to 'Grace to You' with the Bible teaching of John MacArthur . . ."

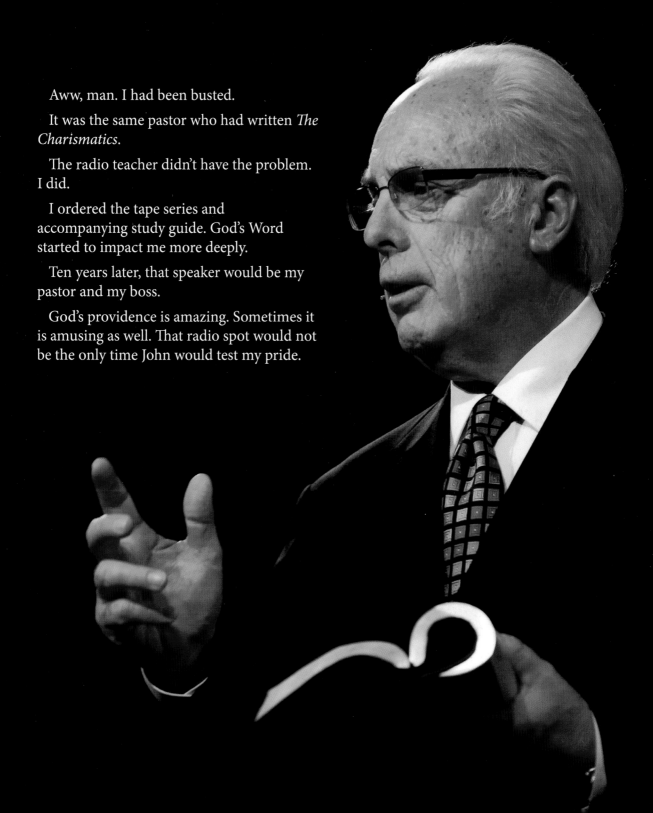

Aww, man. I had been busted.

It was the same pastor who had written *The Charismatics*.

The radio teacher didn't have the problem. I did.

I ordered the tape series and accompanying study guide. God's Word started to impact me more deeply.

Ten years later, that speaker would be my pastor and my boss.

God's providence is amazing. Sometimes it is amusing as well. That radio spot would not be the only time John would test my pride.

The Man of Unassuming Generosity

I have a friend named David (not his real name) who now serves as a pastor on the east coast. Early in our friendship, David told me a story. He was a young and somewhat isolated missionary in England when John MacArthur came to that country for a time of ministry.

David's time was not without difficulty. Men around him in ministry did not live up to the faithfulness that their position should have required.

John spent much time with David on that trip, encouraging him and giving counsel to him—even though David didn't have much to offer in return to a man of John's stature.

No matter. For John, the exchange was not about what he could get.

It was about what he could give.

When the time came for them to part, John spoke some final words of encouragement to his younger friend in ministry. John extended his hand and David shook it.

"I love you, brother," John said.

A strange crinkling sound occurred in the handshake as something passed from John's hand to David's.

John disappeared into the crowd.

David unfolded the paper in his hands.

Money. Lots of it. Three hundred British pounds (about US $600 at the time) to be exact.

A gift from John MacArthur, who understood that money doesn't come easily to a missionary on the field, and who loved enough to give generously from his own resources (not needing a receipt for tax purposes, mind you) to help a brother who had nothing to offer him in return.

Grace to You, John MacArthur's media ministry, hired me for a part-time counseling position in their counseling department on July 25, 1996.

My work station at 24900 Anza Drive in Valencia, California was quite modest. I had a small cubicle in a high-traffic area with a desktop computer.

Ten feet away from my desk sat Melinda MacArthur, who worked on the web page at the time. Proximity guaranteed that we would get to know each other.

The job went on and I started feeling pretty good about myself. I was a former attorney, a good seminary student, and I worked for JOHN MACARTHUR.

At some point, I suppose, Melinda mentioned me to her high-profile parents. I'm sure it was kind and positive. We had a lot of laughs back then.

Well, at last providence brought all of it together. My elevation into John MacArthur's orbit was about to be made complete.

After an evening service, I "chanced" upon John and Patricia MacArthur in the parking lot of Grace Community Church. Everything that follows happened in about ten seconds, but the key thing for the present story is this: My Moment Had Arrived.

Patricia greeted me warmly and then she began speaking to John.

"John, this is Don Green." (Well, of course I'm Don Green. I work for him.)

"You remember. I said we should have a meal together." (Yes! The INNER CIRCLE is just ahead!)

The blank look on John's face instantly told me the conversation was going awry.

I was in the middle of a future Southwest Airlines commercial.

"Wanna get away?"

"Oh yes, I remember," John said rather blandly. "Melinda did mention you

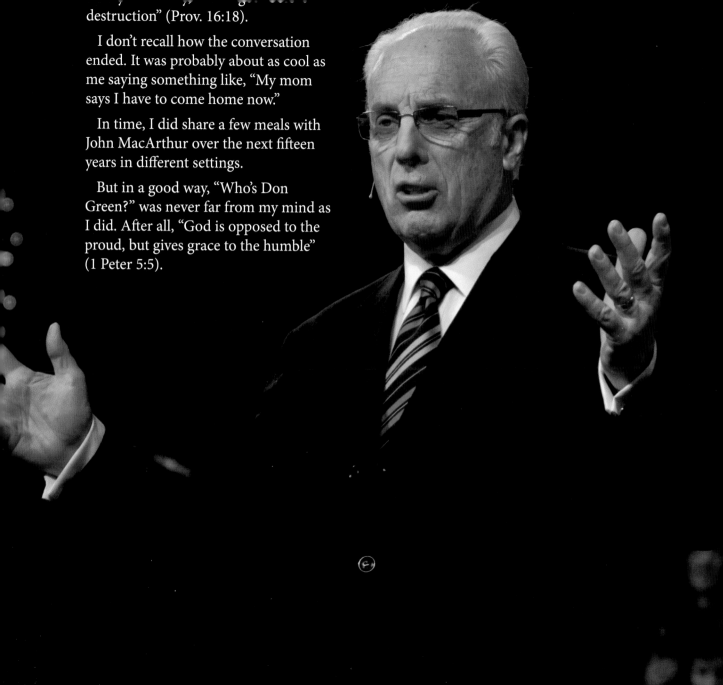

destruction" (Prov. 16:18).

I don't recall how the conversation ended. It was probably about as cool as me saying something like, "My mom says I have to come home now."

In time, I did share a few meals with John MacArthur over the next fifteen years in different settings.

But in a good way, "Who's Don Green?" was never far from my mind as I did. After all, "God is opposed to the proud, but gives grace to the humble" (1 Peter 5:5).

J ohn MacArthur taught me about leadership.

His track record at Grace Community Church, Grace to You, The Master's University, The Master's Seminary, his writings, and other things too numerous to mention establishes conclusively that John knows how to lead people and organizations effectively.

To sit under his teaching is one thing, and is obviously the way most people "know" him.

To work under him is something different. He has a unique style of leadership that takes time and patience to grasp.

Phil Johnson promoted me into the administration of Grace to You in 1999. In time, I became the managing director and held that position until I left Grace to You in April 2012.

It's not from false modesty that I say this: I was not a natural fit for secondary leadership responsibilities in a John MacArthur organization. I was a former attorney, trained to do things by the book. My prior career taught me to anticipate problems and prevent them.

Caution and planning were key tools of the profession.

I was a bean counter.

decisive. Out of nature and necessity, he makes quick decisions that sometimes he will change later. "The key to leadership is good second decisions," I recall him saying.

When he reverses course, you need to go with the flow, not object with, "You said the opposite last month."

It's no insult to John's stature to say that, at times, that frustrated me. I wasn't wired that way.

John taught me I needed to change through his book *Twelve Ordinary Men* (W Publishing Group, 2002). What he wrote about Philip stopped me cold (pp. 121, 125):

> It seems Philip was a classic "process person." He was a facts-and-figures guy—a by-the-book, practical-minded, non-forward-thinking type of individual. He was the kind who tends to be a corporate killjoy, pessimistic, narrowly focused, sometimes missing the big picture, often obsessed with identifying reasons things can't be done rather than finding ways to do them. He was predisposed to be a pragmatist and a cynic—and sometimes a defeatist—rather than a visionary.

Whether officially or unofficially, he seems to have been the one who was always concerned with organization and protocol. He was the type of person who in every meeting says, "I don't think we can do that"—the master of the impossible. And apparently, as far as he was concerned, almost everything fit into that category.

THAT was hard to read, even though John didn't aim it at me (as far as I know!). I moped about that for days. "I'm just trying to do things properly and in order!" But eventually I came to realize: as usual, John was right.

His book held a mirror to me. I was initially a Philip at Grace to You. I'm sure John saw that in me even though he graciously never said a word about it.

The fact that I didn't like what I saw wasn't John's fault. I needed to change if I had aspirations for a greater sphere of leadership.

There are wistful moments when I wonder what would have happened in my ministry if I were more like John and less like Philip. That question is unanswerable.

But the fact I even ask it shows the single most strategic lesson about leadership that I personally gained from John. It came from a book, yes, but even more from his life.

Great leaders don't manage process.

They influence people.

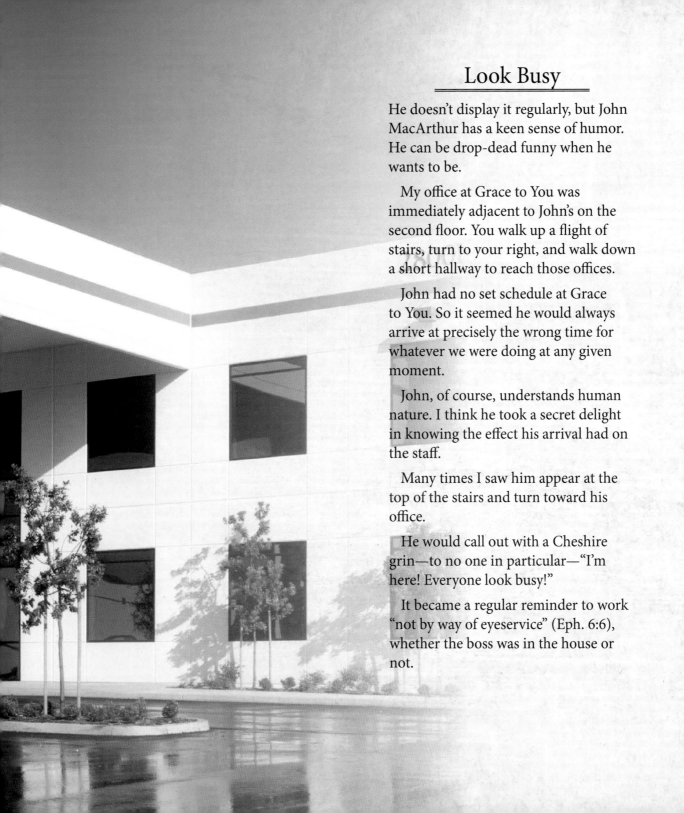

Look Busy

He doesn't display it regularly, but John MacArthur has a keen sense of humor. He can be drop-dead funny when he wants to be.

My office at Grace to You was immediately adjacent to John's on the second floor. You walk up a flight of stairs, turn to your right, and walk down a short hallway to reach those offices.

John had no set schedule at Grace to You. So it seemed he would always arrive at precisely the wrong time for whatever we were doing at any given moment.

John, of course, understands human nature. I think he took a secret delight in knowing the effect his arrival had on the staff.

Many times I saw him appear at the top of the stairs and turn toward his office.

He would call out with a Cheshire grin—to no one in particular—"I'm here! Everyone look busy!"

It became a regular reminder to work "not by way of eyeservice" (Eph. 6:6), whether the boss was in the house or not.

The Family Man

Some have the impression that John MacArthur is an unbending man based on their misguided perceptions of him based solely on his pulpit ministry. That impression is not only wrong. It is dreadfully wrong.

The truth is John MacArthur is kind and unfailingly gracious in his private interactions. Brief moments sometimes tell it best.

John has a private area at Grace Community Church to which he retires between the Sunday morning services. It's a touch of quiet in the midst of very public responsibilities.

I was at Grace on January 15, 2017. A friend in the security department had arranged for me to meet John between the services.

I was ushered to this private place and walked in. For a few seconds, John was not aware of my presence. I'm glad. It allowed me to see a simple but profound moment.

John was sitting in a chair. One of his young granddaughters was standing before him—perfectly comfortable in the presence of the man she simply knows as her grandpa.

She had her mouth opened wide. She had a loose tooth to show him.

The internationally known pastor and best-selling author smiled at her. "Here, let me help you with that." He wiggled the tooth for a moment with tender compassion. Soon she was on her happy way.

It was a picture of our gracious Lord, who in the midst of busy ministry, wanted the children to come to Him (Mark 10:13-16).

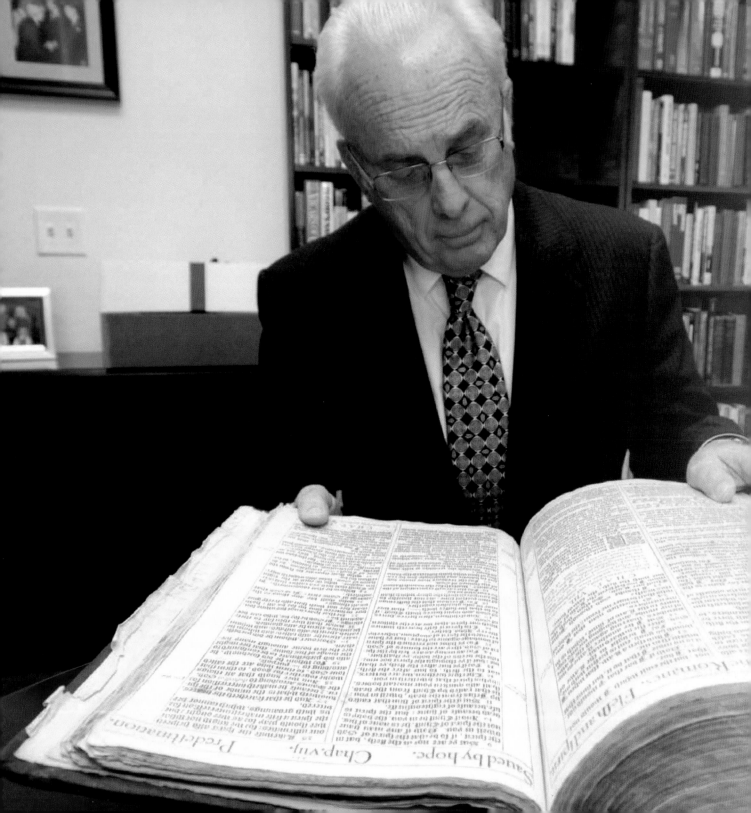

A Fellow Elder

Here's another humorous memory of my time with John MacArthur. John was instrumental in having me affirmed as an elder at Grace Community Church in 2004.

At the time, the Grace elders met monthly in a large classroom on campus. Several tables were joined together in an inward-looking square to seat the 30-35 elders. We usually sat in the same places although the seats were not assigned.

John always sat in the southwest corner of that square. I sat immediately to his left.

From that position, he would often whisper insights to me privately or ask for background information pertaining to the discussion.

But it wasn't always deep or theological. Sometimes it was just ordinary or downright funny.

One time, another elder was introducing another man for an important position.

The elder had made a fundamental error—a rookie mistake, really.

He didn't tell John first.

So picture the scene. The presenter is waxing eloquently about the new man and his giftedness. Surely he was destined for greatness.

In the midst of the fawning, John—whose opinion is obviously first among equals on such matters—leans over to me. With a mixture of exasperation and curiosity, he softly asks me, "Who IS that guy?"

I shrugged and said something like, "No clue."

We shared a quiet laugh about the pretensions of men.

No one else was wise to the moment.

A Shepherd at Heart

History will understandably speak about John MacArthur primarily as a Bible teacher. That picture, while accurate, will be incomplete.

John MacArthur is also an exemplary pastor who is faithful to his flock.

He makes hospital visits. He officiates funerals.

He gives private counsel. He makes calls to those in need.

One such occasion was November 17, 2008. Bob (not his real name), a young employee at The Master's College, had a massive heart attack and was pronounced dead at Henry Mayo Newhall Hospital a short time later.

Bob had become my close friend. I was shocked when I was called to the hospital.

When I arrived, John MacArthur was already there with Bob's wife (Heather) and others. He was just about to leave.

Duty done, John was headed home, right?

Wrong. John MacArthur is a pastor.

John (and others) took Heather and her children home.

Nancy and I came later. I watched John MacArthur the pastor. He was a comforting but not dominating presence during that time.

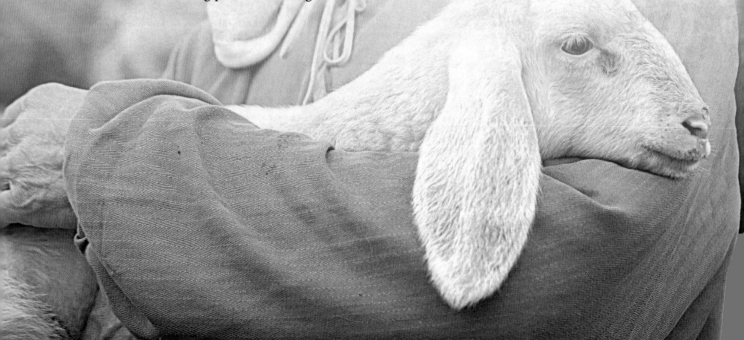

He spoke kindly to the family. He interacted calmly and sympathetically with all the guests.

A few days later, he conducted the funeral.

So NOW he was finished, right? NOW he moved on?

No. Don't you get it? John MacArthur is a pastor.

In the following days, he often reached out to Heather and the children before they relocated to another city to move on with their lives.

That's one story of his pastoral care. There are countless more stories like it.

When I am perplexed in ministry, I often ask myself, "What would John do?"

The answer guides me. Because John MacArthur is, in the highest sense, *a pastor.*

On September 18, 2011, I stood in the pulpit of Grace Community Church at both morning services, holding a great piece of history, and made a special presentation to John MacArthur.

Here's what I said. It's self-explanatory:

Our minds are not accustomed to transcendence. God has ordained that we chiefly glorify Him in the routine of life: whether you eat or drink or whatever you do, do all to the glory of God.

But this is a transcendent day as we recognize how God has honored this pulpit.

On February 9, 1969, John MacArthur began teaching at Grace Community Church. On June 5, 2011, he finished teaching through all 7,955 verses of the New Testament.

How can we measure the human significance of this achievement?

Here's one way. In 1969, a portion of John's congregation had been born in the nineteenth century. He now preaches to young people born in the twenty-first century. If the Lord tarries, some of them will be saying in the twenty-second century, "I heard John MacArthur preach in person."

How can we measure the spiritual significance of this achievement?

At one level, our love for the Word of God, both written and

Incarnate, has increased. At another level, only eternity will unfold the ramifications of John's ministry.

In this brief moment on September 18, 2011, we pause to recognize the transcendent.

God has done something in our midst almost unique in the 2000-year history of Christianity: a comprehensive exposition of the New Testament through the voice of one man in one church.

John MacArthur has been His instrument.

I am here to present a gift on behalf of the Grace to You Board of Directors, the Grace to You staff, and our worldwide audience. John, please come.

To be clear: we are marking a milestone, not the finish line. The best is yet to come.

What gift is worthy of this occasion? Only one.

Exactly 400 years ago, a London printer named Robert Barker released a work now described as "the noblest monument of English prose," "a landmark in the history of the English language," and "the most influential book in the history of English civilization."

John, in honor of your achievement, it is my privilege to present you with this original, first edition, first issue copy of the 1611 King James Bible.

On behalf of Grace to You and countless believers around the world: Congratulations and God bless you.

A Pastor to John MacArthur

John MacArthur is gracious to a fault. I was on the receiving end of his kindness more times than I can remember.

One such time was in the 2009 release of the second volume of his devotional, *Daily Readings from the Life of Christ* (Moody Publishers, 2009). Allowing rhetoric to surpass reality, he dedicated it as follows:

> To Don Green, a friend, uniquely gifted as a strong and wise scholar, teacher, counselor, and leader.

Shortly after that book was released, John went into the hospital for some difficult surgery.

Now when John even sneezes, thousands of people gather around to say, "Bless you."

You can only guess at the chaos when something is more serious.

Understandably, the family said, "No visitors, please." The alternative was for John to entertain people in his hospital room when he simply needed to rest.

But people in the hospital should at least get pastoral visits, even if the public is sent away.

What happens when the pastor is the patient? Who ministers to him?

At the time, I was a pastor in one of the adult fellowship groups at Grace. I knew the patient. So I had a duty. I intended to fulfill it, even if it was John MacArthur.

I drove to St. John's Health Center in Santa Monica and found my way to his room. I had no idea what to expect when I got there.

I gently opened the door, peeked in, and saw him lying in his bed with Patricia standing at his side.

Patricia—warm and approachable as ever—smiled and welcomed me in.

I stood with her at the bedside of him.

John MacArthur.

They had said, "No visitors." But if John didn't want me there, he sure fooled me in the moment.

He was genuinely glad to see me.

Standing at his side, I said "Well, John, if you're going to call me a 'friend,' this is what you get. Friends see each other in their time of need."

It wouldn't be appropriate for me to lift the veil on the private conversation that followed.

It was brief. It was sweet. It was special.

I read Scripture and prayed for them. I took my leave, and made my way back to my car in the California sun.

In one sense, it was a routine pastoral call.

In another sense, it was a unique gift from God to me.

For a few short moments, I was a pastor to John MacArthur.

And he and Patricia received me like I belonged there.

Like I was a friend.

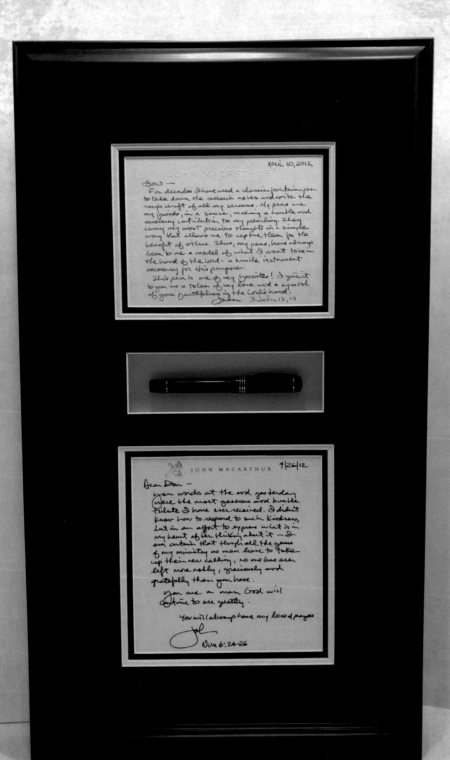

My preferred writing instrument is a $2.00 gel pen from Walmart.

John MacArthur is a lover of fine fountain pens. He uses them to record his research and write his sermon notes. That matters for this story.

When I resigned from Grace to You to move to my new ministry in Cincinnati, it was determined that my last day on the job would be April 13, 2012.

John called me a few days beforehand to schedule a private lunch. He said earnestly, "There are so many things on my heart I need to say to you."

We went to Macaroni Grill in Valencia on April 10. It was one of his favorite lunch spots. So it was a familiar setting as the two of us sat toward the back.

We had eaten there many times together, with or without others present.

A Pen As We Part

But this was different. He was no longer my boss or formally my pastor. It's hard to say what we were as we sat together.

I won't say we were peers. John MacArthur has no peers.

I guess I was a soldier sitting with my general, reminiscing over past battles.

Providence had aligned our paths for nearly two decades. Now, providence was leading us apart.

I told him it was momentous to move out from his teaching and authority. I didn't do it lightly. He supported and affirmed the move.

I wouldn't call John MacArthur "sentimental." But he came prepared for the moment.

He pulled a small bag out of his pocket. "Here, I want you to have this."

An expensive fountain pen was inside. "It's the one I used to prepare my notes on Isaiah 53."

I used it only once—to write the notes for my remarks at my farewell party at Grace to You a few days later.

Then I had it framed. It hangs prominently in my study. It looks over my left shoulder daily as I do my own sermon preparation.

It once served a far greater man and preacher than me.

Now the pen silently reminds me of the many blessed years I spent in the shadow of its former master.

Farewell for Now

For over ten years in my role at Grace to You, I led staff meetings on a near-weekly basis. Over the years, they were routine, fun, challenging, encouraging, informative, or even sad.

What can I say?

We lived life together with a common purpose: to teach biblical truth with clarity, taking advantage of various means of mass communications to expand the sphere of John MacArthur's teaching ministry.

But on April 25, 2012, roles were reversed. I was on the receiving end of a staff meeting. It was a formal farewell luncheon in my honor.

Nancy and our kids were present as various staff members shared memories about my time with them. To this day I cherish what my friends and colleagues did for me that day.

There was just one problem with all that kindness: John MacArthur was in the audience. An underling like me should not be the center of attention.

As so happens at these events, I had opportunity to say a few words at the end. I had scribbled a few handwritten notes with the fountain pen John had given me. This is what I said:

> Nancy and I, along with our kids, will remember this day as long as we live. Thank you for this tremendous love and generosity.

> Look. What gives this meaning is our common life in Christ. This would not be the same at all if we were a group of unbelievers working in a factory some place. Christ is the one who makes this meaningful to us, so we give all the glory to Him.

> There are thousands of people around the world who would like to do what I've done these past fifteen years, which is to work on this staff under the leadership of John MacArthur.

> *(I removed the pen John had given to me, held it up, and looked at him.)*

> John, this token of our friendship is priceless to me.

> As I was walking the dirt roads in Acton (our hometown in California) yesterday, thinking about what I would say, a thought alarmed me.

> Grace to You is unique in its exclusive devotion to John MacArthur. The church,

college, and seminary all have broader purposes.

John MacArthur will probably never retire from Grace to You. There may never be an opportunity to honor *him* in this kind of focused manner at Grace to You. That wouldn't be right.

Slaves should not be honored over their master.

The millions of people who follow and support Grace to You don't do so for the managing director.

So on a day when we are really celebrating the ministry of Grace to You, there's only one place where the attention should be focused.

John, in case there is never an event like this for you at Grace to You, because you will never leave, I want to say this.

As my final act with the staff of Grace to You, we honor you.

Generations yet to be born will call us blessed because we had the privilege of serving Christ at this profound ministry.

You are our pastor, leader, and friend. You are gracious in your oversight and generous in your care for us. We thank God for you.

God bless you, our pastor, both now and forevermore.

We applauded John. I sat down.

Fifteen years of my life ended on April 25, 2012 as my new life in Cincinnati was about to begin. I would no longer have the ongoing access to John. But his imprint on my life would be manifest in my future ministry.

I realize some cynics may scorn this book as excessive praise from a friend of a well-known pastor. That doesn't concern me. I'm more concerned that future generations will criticize me for my restraint in not having said more.

So why write this book? It is sufficient to remember that Scripture speaks often of the honor that should be given to older Christians, especially those in ministry.

"Who honors those who fear the LORD" (Ps. 15:4).

"You shall rise up before the gray-headed and honor the aged, and you shall revere your God; I am the LORD" (Lev. 19:32).

"Do not sharply rebuke an older man, but rather appeal to him as a father" (1 Tim. 5:1).

"The elders who rule well are to be considered worthy of double honor, especially those who work hard at preaching and teaching" (1 Tim. 5:17).

"Remember those who led you, who spoke the word of God to you, and considering the result of their conduct, imitate their faith" (Heb.13:7).

"Obey your leaders and submit to them, for they keep watch over your souls as those who will give an account. Let them do this with joy and not with grief, for this would be unprofitable to you" (Heb. 13:17).

As I write this book, John MacArthur is eighty-two years old. You think he doesn't somehow feel that when he climbs in or out of bed each day? Yet he is still serving as the pastor of Grace Community Church, preaching on a regular basis, leading multiple organizations, giving high profile interviews, resisting government interference with the church, and providing leadership to the broader Christian community on significant matters affecting the church.

I'm grateful to the Lord for giving John health so that his influence can continue. He is fighting battles at an age when most are either dead, enjoying retirement, or under nursing care. Most of his fellow soldiers from his generation have already gone to heaven: James Montgomery Boice, R. C. Sproul, and D. James Kennedy, just to name a few. John is the last man standing of that great generation of pulpit voices.

I'm quite sure Christ is strengthening him, renewing his inner man day by day in anticipation of an eternal reward far beyond all comparison to the present earthly labor (2 Cor. 4:16-18). But John MacArthur is not indestructible. He's human. Life is fleeting. Our gracious Lord will eventually receive him to his heavenly reward.

For those with ears to hear, I ask you to play the part of a loving and discerning Christian. Realize that in John MacArthur, God has given us a man for the ages. The subject matter of his many books shows that John has vindicated the Word of God against every attack that rose against it during his ministry.

It is difficult to think of any major biblical issue from the past fifty years that he has not addressed with clarity, conviction, and without apology for the Bible. For example, he has upheld

Scripture on the doctrine of salvation (*The Gospel According to Jesus*), the attack of psychology (*Our Sufficiency in Christ*), the errors of the charismatic movement (*Charismatic Chaos; Strange Fire*), postmodernism (*Why One Way?*), the seeker-sensitive philosophy of ministry (*Ashamed of the Gospel*), the postmodern, emergent church movement (*The Truth War*), and biblical creation (*The Battle for the Beginning*). Anyone familiar with his work knows that I've only given a sample with that list.

That is all in addition to the expositional work of *The MacArthur Study Bible*, the detailed exposition of the New Testament in *The MacArthur New Testament Commentary* series, and his work of systematic theology, *Biblical Doctrine*.

His timeless body of work will be serving future Christians long after we are all gone.

John MacArthur has shown us the high excellence of Scripture and the exalted majesty of the Lord Jesus Christ.

It is biblical to observe deeply and take it to heart.

On a personal level, I'm grateful for John's

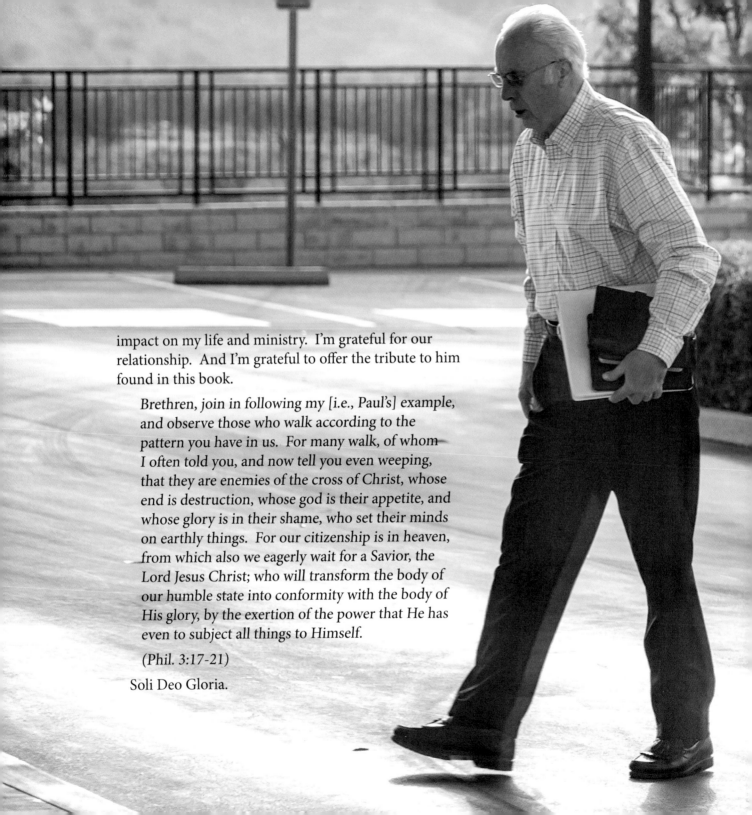

impact on my life and ministry. I'm grateful for our relationship. And I'm grateful to offer the tribute to him found in this book.

Brethren, join in following my [i.e., Paul's] example, and observe those who walk according to the pattern you have in us. For many walk, of whom I often told you, and now tell you even weeping, that they are enemies of the cross of Christ, whose end is destruction, whose god is their appetite, and whose glory is in their shame, who set their minds on earthly things. For our citizenship is in heaven, from which also we eagerly wait for a Savior, the Lord Jesus Christ; who will transform the body of our humble state into conformity with the body of His glory, by the exertion of the power that He has even to subject all things to Himself.

(Phil. 3:17-21)

Soli Deo Gloria.

A John MacArthur Reading Plan

Awhile back, I develped a reading plan for others to use to give them broad exposure to books by John MacArthur. It consists of a dozen of his major feature books from over the years. I share the list with you in case you would like to do it, also:

1. The Gospel According to Jesus

2. The Gospel According to the Apostles

3. Our Sufficiency in Christ

4. Ashamed of the Gospel

5. The Vanishing Conscience

6. The Battle for the Beginning

7. The Freedom and Power of Forgiveness

8. The Truth War

9. Twelve Ordinary Men

10. Strange Fire

11. The Gospel According to Paul

12. The Glory of Heaven

The sequence is deliberate, mixing didactic, polemic, and pastoral books with a culmination in a study of heaven—precisely where our souls will arrive when our work on earth is done.

At the attainable rate of one per month, the reader will have John's biblical thought and discernment impressed deeply on his mind.

And now I commend you to God and to the word of His grace, which is able to build you up and to give you the inheritance among all those who are sanctified.
(Acts 20:32)

JOHN MACARTHUR

FIGHTING for CERTAINTY in an Age of Deception

THE TRUTH War

JOHN MACARTHUR

STRANGE FIRE

The Danger of Offending the Holy Spirit with Counterfeit Worship

REVISED & EXPANDED ANNIVERSARY EDITION

JOHN MACARTHUR

THE GOSPEL ACCORDING TO JESUS

JOHN MACARTHUR

THE Glory OF HEAVEN

OUR SUFFICIENCY IN CHRIST   MACARTHUR

THE FREEDOM AND POWER OF FORGIVENESS   MACARTHUR

The Battle for the Beginning   JOHN MACARTHUR

THE VANISHING CONSCIENCE   JOHN F. MACARTHUR, JR.

THE GOSPEL ACCORDING TO THE APOSTLES   John MacArthur

TWELVE ORDINARY MEN   JOHN MAC...

ASHAMED OF THE GOSPEL

WHEN THE CHURCH BECOMES LIKE THE WORLD

JOHN F. MACARTHUR JR.

EMBRACING THE GOOD NEWS AT THE HEART OF PAUL'S TEACHINGS

THE GOSPEL ACCORDING TO PAUL

JOHN MACARTHUR

BESTSELLING AUTHOR OF TWELVE ORDINARY MEN

In 2018, I twice had the privilege of hosting John MacArthur at Truth Community Church, the church I pastor in Cincinnati, Ohio. On both occasions, I interviewed him live in front of our congregation. In the pages that follow, you'll find lightly edited transcripts of our dialogues. The personal anecdotes, combined with his incisive observations about the condition of the twenty-first-century church, make for highly edifying and enjoyable reading.

It's my privilege now to introduce our speaker this evening. Our speaker tonight is the President of the Master's University and the Master's Seminary. I'm a graduate of the Master's Seminary, but that's not why our speaker is here this evening.

Our speaker tonight is the featured teacher on "Grace to You," the worldwide Bible teaching program that is heard by millions each day. I served at Grace to You for fifteen years, but that's not why our speaker is here this evening.

Our speaker tonight is the author of the best-selling *The MacArthur Study Bible,* the complete *MacArthur New Testament Commentary* series, and scores of other biblical books and theological resources. I consult his work regularly in my pulpit preparation here at Truth Community Church, but that's not why our speaker is here this evening, either.

Our speaker tonight is the pastor of Grace Community Church in Sun Valley, California, where he has served continuously since 1969. There have been eight United States presidents since the prior pastor served at Grace Community Church. Next February will mark his fiftieth anniversary in that pastorate. My personal opinion is this (and I was around long enough that I think I'm entitled to an opinion on this matter) no one has begun to understand our speaker tonight until they realize that he is first and foremost a pastor. He preaches God's Word to the same flock over time. He leads elders. He makes hospital visits. He officiates funerals. He gives counsel. I've watched him personally in every one of those roles multiple times. He loves his flock and, boy, does his flock love him.

That's why our speaker is here tonight. We want to hear from a shepherd of Christ's flock. If I were half the pastor that our speaker is, I'd be ten times the pastor that I am. Please join me in welcoming to our platform Pastor John MacArthur.

No one has begun to understand our speaker tonight until they realize that he is first and foremost a pastor. He preaches God's Word to the same flock over time. He leads elders. He makes hospital visits. He officiates funerals. He gives counsel.

John: Thank you very much. Those were such kind words. Would you do my funeral?

Don: It was kind of like an audition.

John: Okay.

Don: But I'm hoping that funeral is not for another thirty years, John.

John: Thank you.

Don: You have been preaching God's Word for sixty years, not just in the fifty years at Grace Church, you were ministering God's Word ten years prior to that, and I suppose this is kind of a funny way to ask the question but don't you ever get tired of it? What keeps you motivated after all of those years speaking God's Word?

The Word of God is alive. It is powerful. It is a living book. The Father has glory, the Son has glory, the Spirit has glory, and all Their glory is reflected in the Scripture. It just explodes with its glory on my mind and my soul.

John: There isn't any sense at all in which this is wearying, old, stale. The Word of God is alive. It is powerful. It is a living book. The Father has glory, the Son has glory, the Spirit has glory, and all Their glory is reflected in the Scripture. It just explodes with its glory on my mind and my soul. There is as much joy in preparation now, and I just preached my fiftieth Easter sermon, there is as much joy now as there was at the very beginning. It has never diminished.

Part of that, of course, is related not just to the content of Scripture which is inexhaustible, but to the Lord of Scripture, the unfathomable glory of the Lord. I never can get enough of Christ. Well, as you know, all those years through Matthew, Mark, Luke, John, and then the people said, "Could you go back through John again?" So we did that again and then they said, "Do a series on Christ in the Old Testament." So we did that. The Old Testament is the anticipation of Christ; the Gospels, the Incarnation of Christ; the book of Acts, the proclamation of Christ; the epistles, the explanation of Christ; and the book of Revelation, the glorification of Christ; and even He, in Luke 24, went to the Old Testament and explained the things concerning Himself. I find Christ everywhere in Scripture and you can never get enough of Him. After all, we're going to spend the entire eternity gazing at His glory and I think we're just seeing the outer edges now.

Don: "The Word Incarnate" and "the Word written" become sweeter and sweeter the more you get to know them both.

John: Yeah, and I think there is a statement, and you've heard me say this for years, in 1 John where it talks about spiritual babies and spiritual young men and spiritual fathers, 1 John 2: a spiritual baby knows the Father, it's sort of spiritual Dada, there's kind of an entry level understanding, and then a spiritual young man knows doctrine. We are able to defeat the evil one who primarily works in the area of false doctrine, but a spiritual Father knows him who is from the beginning. Long-term study of the Word of God will introduce you to theology and then all of a sudden you will find yourself breaking through theology to the knowledge of God, and that's where the profound joys really are available.

Don: So what I hear you saying is you're going to keep doing this as long as the Lord gives you breath.

John: I do want to do that, and I tell them at the church, "Look, as long as I make sense, leave me there. When I don't make sense, get me out, but realize I won't know I don't make sense. So you might have a fight."

> *I'm fifty years into this and I have seen the Word of God completely design and define and shape a church. Very rare that pastors stay long enough to see that, but you know this, I'm ministering to the third generation.*

Don: John, we spoke briefly a few days ago to prepare for this evening and you said something that really struck me. You said that when you were here, you did not want to be treated as a celebrity pastor. One of the things that you said about ministry comes from 1 Corinthians 4:1: "Regard us as this, servants of Christ and stewards of the mysteries of God." Explain for us how that perspective on ministry in the life of a pastor would shape the life of a local church.

John: You know, the big picture there is I'm fifty years into this and I have seen the Word of God completely design and define and shape a church. Very rare that pastors stay long enough to see that, but you know this, I'm ministering to the third generation. I'm now involved in the spiritual growth of the grandchildren of the people that were there when I came and I am being introduced to the great-grandchildren. What Luther said was so important, he said, "I did nothing, the Word did everything," and you understand that. You know that's what you're doing here. I did nothing. I didn't plan Grace Church. I didn't have some kind of scheme, dream, method. I basically said, "Look, let's just teach the Word of God and see what the Lord does with His Word," and transformed people who love Christ will love each other and they will also be concerned about the lost and the gospel, and they will explode into ministry.

So I never really started ministries, I just watched the Word do its work in transforming lives, and as believers walked with Christ and grew and developed and their gifts became used and refined. You know, I'm at the end of this thing looking back and I never wanted to come to a point in my ministry where I wondered whether I did this or the Lord did this. I will never be the explanation for Grace Church. That's hard for them to get that, in a sense, but you know that. I am not the explanation. This is the explanation. Sometimes people think, "Well, you know, you're kind of doctrinal and kind of firm," and I just want to encourage people: strong preaching makes soft people; soft preaching makes hard people.

> *Strong preaching of the Word of God breaks down*
> *sin and it breaks down self-will, and it breaks down*
> *pride, and it humbles and softens and weakens the*
> *flesh, as the Spirit does His work.*

Don: What do you mean by that? Explain that a little bit.

John: I mean, strong preaching of the Word of God breaks down sin and it breaks down self-will, and it breaks down pride, and it humbles and softens and weakens the flesh, as the Spirit does His work.

Soft preaching that intends to manipulate people emotionally just leaves people in the hardness of their own hearts. So I think one of the surprises that people who come to Grace Church, like when they come to a Shepherds' Conference, they can't believe all the loving, caring service. If they're listening on the radio, you know, they hear me banging away at sound doctrine and the strong conviction. So all I've ever done is explain what the Bible meant to the people. Just, "This is what the Bible means," and in fact, you know I've never really been so much caught up in the application as the implication. Scripture has so much weight of its own that if you just place an accurate interpretation of a passage on someone's back who is a believer, the weight of that alone drives application in many directions.

I have to hold the other reality that a weak, ignorant, entertainment-centered church is not going to be the instrument that the Lord can use in a maximum level and is going to be very likely to produce half-Christians who are not genuinely converted.

Image credit: Ligonier.org

Don: Now, kind of building on your longevity in ministry, you preached not too long ago at the memorial service for R. C. Sproul, spoke for maybe about ten minutes or so, and you made a comment in that that really stood out to me. There was a poignancy to it related to your own ministry. You spoke about a meeting that you had with R. C. and a few other leaders: J. I. Packer, Bill Bright, D. James Kennedy, and Charles Colson. You made the point that the other five of those had gone on to glory and you used the phrase, "I'm the last man standing," at least of that group. You have lived long enough and been in ministry long enough where a lot of your contemporaries have gone on to the Lord. I think of James Montgomery Boice, a man that we both respected, and as I thought about that, I wanted to ask you this: you've seen a generation come and go; you see another generation of preachers coming up behind you. Tell us your perspective on how

Christ builds His church over the ages and the enduring power of Christ to fulfill His promise in Matthew 16, "I will build My church."

John: Christ will build His church. He will accomplish it. He has chosen in eternity past and He said, "All that the Father gives to Me will come to Me and I will lose none of them but raise them at the last day." The Lord will build His church, that strong confidence in the sovereign purpose of God.

However, on the other hand, I think it's not a guarantee that the church is going to be strong, and I have to hold the other reality that a weak, ignorant, entertainment-centered church is not going to be the instrument that the Lord can use in a maximum level and is going to be very likely to produce half-Christians who are not genuinely converted. So I fear for the character of the church in the broad sense, and yet I have confidence in God's purposes. Now, I hold that tension in all theology. I am deeply burdened at what goes on in pulpits and what goes on in the name of Christ in churches.

So my passion, and you know this, is to raise up men who will do ministry biblically for the honor of the Lord, for the clarity of doctrine, for the sake of the advance of the kingdom, and for their own joy.

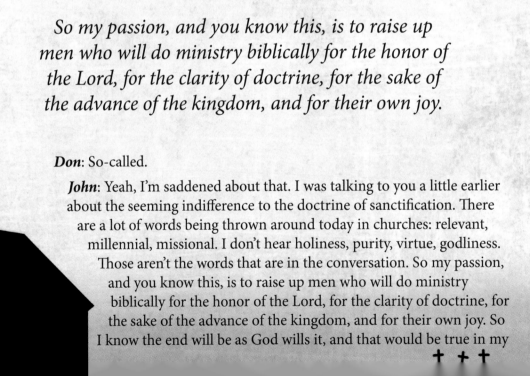

Don: So-called.

John: Yeah, I'm saddened about that. I was talking to you a little earlier about the seeming indifference to the doctrine of sanctification. There are a lot of words being thrown around today in churches: relevant, millennial, missional. I don't hear holiness, purity, virtue, godliness. Those aren't the words that are in the conversation. So my passion, and you know this, is to raise up men who will do ministry biblically for the honor of the Lord, for the clarity of doctrine, for the sake of the advance of the kingdom, and for their own joy. So I know the end will be as God wills it, and that would be true in my life. That gives me no excuse to sin, and I don't think the church has any excuse for being anything less than God has designed it to be, and a shepherd for being anything less than God has designed him to be. And I think, and we're talking about students that come to The Master's University, Christian students, years ago they had biblical knowledge, they had sort of a general biblical knowledge, they grew up in the church. Today, they come from churches and have virtually no biblical knowledge. I don't know what's going on in their churches but they don't know the Bible. We grew up in church Sunday school listening to Bible stories; most of these contemporary churches have no Sunday school. They have nothing like that. They are just events.

> *I don't think the church has any excuse for being anything less than God has designed it to be, and a shepherd for being anything less than God has designed him to be.*

So this is a scary time and here's the downside, one of the downsides, is you've got all these places and all these leaders claiming to be Christians and about every other day one of them crashes and burns in some kind of moral catastrophe which brings reproach on the name of Jesus Christ, and these are people who had no business ever being in those positions. So I'm not a doomsdayer in that sense, Don, you know. I know the Lord triumphs in the end but that gives us no excuse to be less than what He would want us to be for His honor.

Don: Thank you, John. That kind of leads into something else that I wanted you just to kind of expand on. I think that if you have a high view of Christ, you will necessarily have a high view of the church. Ephesians 5: "Christ loved the church and gave Himself up for her." Galatians 2:20: "He loved me and gave Himself up for me." A high view of Christ leads to a high view of His people. Talk to us a little bit about the love of Christ for His own; let's kind of narrow it down more to the true church, to true Christians, about the love of Christ that sent Him to the cross, and then what that means for His people as we look to Him as we walk through this fallen world.

John: Okay, you just opened up a theological range.

Don: Good. We can be here all night, so go for it.

John: Okay, so this is how to think about that, okay? Ephesians says, "You were chosen in Him before the foundation of the world." You and I and the bride of Christ have been in Christ since eternity past. You were chosen in Christ. This is a stunning reality. In the mind of God and for the purposes of God, for His eternal glory, you were in Christ before the foundation of the world. Your union with Him started then in eternity past and it goes through eternity future. This is the dominating New Testament language to define a Christian: Christ in you, you in Christ. Now, that's Galatians 2:20, "I am crucified with Christ, nevertheless I live," which means I am raised with Christ, "yet not I, but Christ lives in me: and the life which I live in the flesh I live by faith in the Son of God who loved me and gave Himself for me." I don't know where Christ ends and I begin and that's why Paul in 1 Corinthians 6 says, "I can't indulge in a sin without joining Christ to that sin."

I think the missing reality in Christianity today is that Christ is not just someone I believe in; Christ is my life. He is my love. He is my life and He is your life and when you come to me, Christ comes to me. That's how I treat another believer and Matthew 18 is so important because I'm treating him and treating Christ at the same time.

So I think the heart and soul of Christian love is to be literally engulfed in this incomprehensible grace gift of having been Christ's from before the foundation of the world. And I love this little phrase: even when you die, you'll be the dead in Christ. When your body is in the grave, it's still the dead in Christ. Your spirit is alive with Him but that body is still Christ's. You are Christ's from eternity past to eternity future. He is our life and that's why Paul says in Galatians 4:19, "I am in labor pains until Christ is formed in you." He doesn't mean He's not there; he means He's there but He needs to fill you out. Or Colossians 1:28 and 29, Paul says, "Warning every man, teaching every man that I may present every man complete in Christ." He's in Christ but I want him to see the fullness of Christ. Paul talks about the fullness of God and the fullness of Christ.

So I think where Christ fills the life, where you see the fullness of Christ, you have the attributes of Christ being made manifest: love, joy, peace, gentleness, faith, goodness, meekness, self-control, all those things by the Spirit of Christ.

The goal of the shepherd is to see a congregation that looks like Christ. Even as a teacher and a pastor, I should demonstrate the meekness and gentleness of Christ. I should reflect the mind of Christ. It's all about Him. What Christ wants to do to you is exalt Himself through you and then you become fruitful and then there is joy.

People used to say to me, "Why don't you go and do something else? You've done all this in this one congregation, why don't you go and do something else?" There are lots of people in our church in whom Christ is not fully formed and that's my flock that God gave me. That's not a job for me, that's my life. And Christ in me and Christ in them has created a love relationship that continues to grow and flourish, and after this many years, I can just tell you this: it's more wonderful and fulfilling now for all of us than it ever has been in the past because it grows and it just continues to flourish.

There are lots of people in our church in whom Christ is not fully formed and that's my flock that God gave me. That's not a job for me, that's my life.

Don: Deeper all the way.

John: It does. No question.

Don: Now, two more questions because we want to leave all the time. . . .

John: Yeah, leave me something to say when I get up there. I'll have to go back and prepare all over again.

Don: I think after sixty years you've got a pretty deep well to draw upon. I have confidence in you. John, you wouldn't know this but I know that there are a number of small church pastors, at least compared to Grace Church, small churches that are in the audience tonight, they are friends of mine. I just wanted to give you an opportunity to say a word of encouragement to them as they seek to carry out what you just described in their own flock.

John: Yeah, just know this, it's never about the empty seats; it's always about the occupied ones. You get concerned about the empty ones and you'll forfeit your calling. You're never concerned about the empty seats, it's the occupied seats. But I would just say this, first of all, it's obvious that God prefers small churches to big churches because there are so many more small ones. I remember a young man came to Moody one time and he said, "I have a complaint." He said, "My congregation is too small." To which Moody replied, "Maybe they're as large as you'd like to give account for in the day of judgment." Okay. Because we will give an account.

Don: James 3:1, "Let not many of you become teachers."

John: Hebrews 13 says we're going to give an account. That's frightening to me.

Don: Me too.

John: Yeah, and I want to stay long enough so that I can minimize the trauma. So you should be happy with who you've got and love the occupied seats. Don't worry about the empty seats and the Lord will bring who He will bring. It's about being faithful, "It's required of stewards that a man

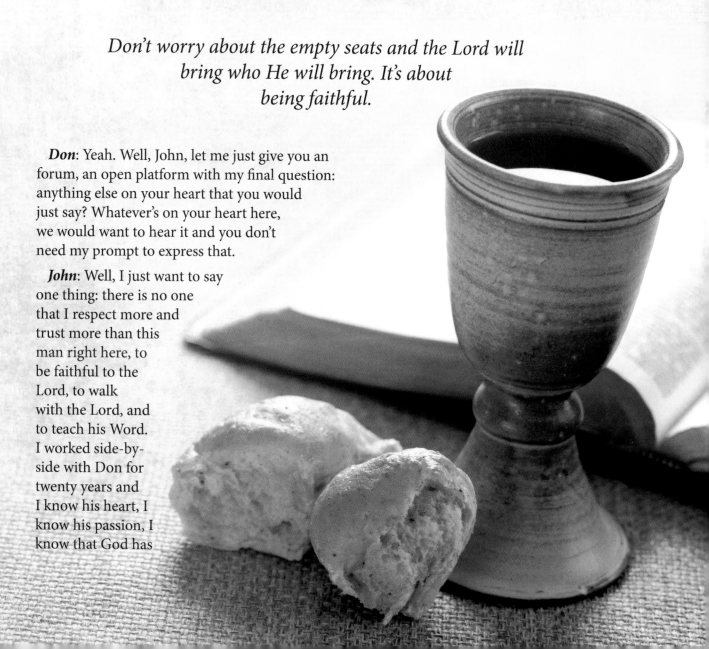

be found faithful." Just be faithful to the truth. Proclaim the truth. You've heard me say this: you take care of the depth of your ministry and let God take care of the breadth of it. You work on the quality of your shepherding and let God take care of the quantity of the sheep. That's His part.

Don't worry about the empty seats and the Lord will bring who He will bring. It's about being faithful.

Don: Yeah. Well, John, let me just give you an forum, an open platform with my final question: anything else on your heart that you would just say? Whatever's on your heart here, we would want to hear it and you don't need my prompt to express that.

John: Well, I just want to say one thing: there is no one that I respect more and trust more than this man right here, to be faithful to the Lord, to walk with the Lord, and to teach his Word. I worked side-by-side with Don for twenty years and I know his heart, I know his passion, I know that God has his hand on him. Finding a trustworthy man is not easy. This is one.

Don: So will you do my funeral?

John: I will. The problem is we've got a reverse order here because, when your funeral comes, I'll be long gone. But I'll come back!

[Laughter]

Don: All right.

John: I'll come back!

October 9, 2018 Interview

In this second interview, John speaks about his family history and his perspective on faithfulness in ministry.

Pastor Don Green: When the Apostle Paul wrote to the church at Philippi, he said, "God is my witness how I long for you all with the affection of Christ Jesus." There is something about the heart of a minister of the gospel that carries affection toward people in his ministry. Our speaker this evening is here at Truth Community Church for the second time in six months. It is a reflection of his affection for Truth Community Church and you can listen in as I say just a word to this friend of ours.

John, we return the affection. You are a friend to us and we want you to know that Truth Community Church is a friend to you as well. Our pulpit is always open to you 24/7, 365 days a year without advance notice. John, as I said to you just a few moments ago, I want to say in the presence of many witnesses, that whatever humanly speaking, whatever happens through my ministry is just derivative of what I have learned from you, from your pulpit, from your books, from your personal example and from our own relationship. It is a wonderful privilege for us to welcome our friend John MacArthur to the platform.

So tell us how you're doing. That's a broad question.

John MacArthur: Well, I haven't had an MRI lately but superficial information is good. I had a physical recently and the doctor said, "Come back in a year." That's pretty good, I guess.

Don: Good.

John: If I don't lose my mind.

Don: You're coming up on your fiftieth anniversary of ministry at Grace Community Church in February. The time has gone by quickly.

John: It's pretty shocking to be marrying the grandchildren of the people that called me to the church. I mean, the third-generation, we are even starting to see the fourth generation.

Don: That's amazing.

John: That's fifty years at Grace Church and my dear wife has said fifty years of enduring my nonstop preaching at home and at church.

Don: And the world is better for that and the church is better as a result of your ministry. Our church, I like to tell people, is a relational church in addition to being centered around the pulpit and so I'd like to share a couple of things relationally from your life that a lot of people may not know. Many people do not know that you had an aborted career as a traffic cop and I was wondering if you might be willing to tell people about that.

John: Well, I had, I guess, latent leadership qualities when I was a little kid. I think I was eight or nine years old when I decided to step into an intersection and stop the traffic. I had seen the policeman do it and it looked like, you know, a good way to exercise your leadership ability, so I stepped into the intersection and I was directing the traffic and I put my hand up as a car drove up and my dad was in that car. I mean, I got a serious whipping.

Don: Dad wasn't excited about your police career.

John: No, no, no, he didn't think that was the career choice for me. You know, my dad had guilt feelings into his later years because he beat me so many times when I deserved it. He broke so many coat hangers and things on me as a kid and that was just one of those moments. I'm deeply indebted to him. I loved him to death, but he loved me enough to discipline me.

I'm deeply indebted to [my dad]. I loved him to death, but he loved me enough to discipline me.

Don: And that's true, the Scripture talks about that, the one who withholds the rod hates his son.

John: He did not spare the rod.

Don: He loved you.

John: He did, a lot, it sounds like. He kept telling me that while he was whipping me.

Don: Now, John, that leads so naturally into one of the things that I wanted to say to you. Your dad, Jack MacArthur, I have my own memories of him of a couple of conversations with him that I cherish, but your dad was a pastor and a preacher; your grandfather, Harry MacArthur, was a man of the Word, a preacher of the Word; Harry's wife, Olivia, her father and her grandfather were pastors. You are the fifth in a line of pastors which is a pretty remarkable legacy to have.

John: Yeah, it is and from all that we can tell going all the way back, they were really faithful preachers of the gospel, men of God. They had great respect from their congregations, great love. My grandfather was really deeply loved by everyone who knew him. He was a very sweet and gracious man and a very faithful man. One of the

treasures that I have is his Bible with all his sermon notes in it that he wrote, and I have his preaching notebook, and I have a whole notebook full of his sermons. He wrote his sermons on the same kind of paper that I write mine on; I think it's genetic, it just gets passed down.

Don: Kind of half-sheet.

John: Yeah.

Don: But you still handwrite your notes to this day, don't you?

John: I do. You remember when *The MacArthur Study Bible* came out, the *Los Angeles Times* said, "Man writes study Bible by hand," like what kind of dinosaur does anything by hand in the computer age. But yeah, I still write. I do all my own sermon research. I write everything into kind of a first draft and then transfer them into notes.

Don: Now I wanted to build on this. You're actually named after. . .

John: My father.

Don: Your father on your first name and your middle name is after your paternal grandmother, Olivia Fullerton. John Fullerton MacArthur. And as I was thinking about that today, anticipating this time, there is a great weight of history given the Fullerton legacy of preaching and the MacArthur legacy of preaching. When you do the math on it, for 150 years to this day there has been an unbroken line of your family that has been pastoring and preaching Scripture. Your thoughts about that.

John: Well, at least that long. Thomas Fullerton, my grandmother's father, was pastor of St. James Kirk which was the large Presbyterian Church in

Charlottetown, Prince Edward Island. He was also a chaplain in the Boer war which meant that he fought with the Canadian troops in South Africa, and he was a friend of the family that wrote *Anne of Green Gables*, that kind of thing.

Don: Lucy Maud Montgomery.

John: Yeah, Lucy Maud Montgomery. That goes back, and then James Stewart, behind him was a Scottish Presbyterian preacher. So yeah, our family has been carrying on the baton for a long time.

I can't find any place in the five generations going back where any of those men did anything that dishonored the Lord. That's the most remarkable thing of all, that the Lord sustained us all with grace, including me.

Don: In fact, John, if the Lord tarries, your books, your audio will be listened to and read for another century if you think about it, and this is a conservative estimate, 250 years of family ministry, that's a quarter of a millennium that will be a reflection of the work of you and your family in ministry. Give us some perspective on that.

John: I never thought of that before. Only you would come up with that. You know, the thing that I marvel about is I can't find any place in the five generations going back where any of those men did anything that dishonored the Lord. That's the most remarkable thing of all, that the Lord sustained us all with grace, including me, and I don't know if my predecessors were as rambunctious as I was as a kid, but yeah, the history is not only of faithful preaching but of, I guess you could say it, an unblemished ministry. There is nothing that ever came up that discredited these men. They served the Lord until the end of their lives. My grandfather had prepared a sermon and he had cancer and he had gone back to the Mayo Clinic and came back and he wasn't going to live, and he had prepared a sermon and the last thing I remember is my father telling me that his father said to him was, "I just wish I could preach one more time," because he had this sermon in his heart. So my dad took his notes, printed them up and passed it out at his funeral and it was a sermon on heaven, so he actually wound up preaching on heaven from heaven. But that's being true to the very very very end; he even prepared a sermon for his own funeral and my dad the same way—he was still teaching the Bible at ninety-one when he went to heaven.

The last thing I remember is my father telling me that his father said to him was, "I just wish I could preach one more time," because he had this sermon in his heart.

Don: The interlocking of generations going back and going forward, it seems to me it's almost a microcosm. Let me put it this way, two things: one is that the stature of your ministry (and I'm not being flattering in saying that, it's just a reality), the stature of your ministry is actually a part of an even bigger story of your family, and your family is simply a reflection of a greater outworking of the eternal plan of God to bring salvation to those who believe in Christ.

John: Yeah, I mean, we're all chosen before the foundation of the world, we're all called with an irresistible call and the Lord just had a path that came down to me and I don't want to put pressure on my two sons, neither of whom felt called into ministry, but have poured their life into serving the Lord in our church, and as you know, they have been board members of Grace to You and faithful to their dad and mom and to honor the Lord in the world that they are in which is the business world, I told them either you preach or you pay the preacher. You know, either you preach or you earn money to support the church, and they have been great. I think early on in their lives they struggled with the fact that they weren't preachers but I was kind of a hard model to follow because it was so intense and I don't think either Matt or Mark could see themselves doing what I was doing. By the time they reached the age where they understood it, I had grown into it from a very small beginning and it sort of came in little increments, but when they looked at it, it just seemed so far beyond that they just poured their life into being a support.

Don: Yeah, there is a sense in which your life in ministry kind of took all the oxygen out of the room.

John: Yeah, I think there's some truth there and I never wanted to put pressure on them. Mostly I wanted them to love Him and serve Him, and they have done that.

Don: Let's go from chronology to geography, if we can. Looking back over your life ministry, you circled the countries in the Pacific Rim in 1988, you spent a lot of time in

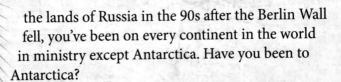

the lands of Russia in the 90s after the Berlin Wall fell, you've been on every continent in the world in ministry except Antarctica. Have you been to Antarctica?

John: I have not. I don't think there's a big work among penguins.

Don: Well, if there was, they would want you to do it, I know that. From your perspective of sixty years of ministry, from all of the opportunities that you've had to preach to the people of God and to evangelize all around the world, give us some perspective, you can take this where you want, on the global body of Christ, on the power of Christ to save men from every tongue, tribe and nation. Just give us some reflection from your perspective as an elder statesman in the church.

I don't think there's a big work among penguins.

John: Well, I think we all know that life comes really fast and I don't really see what's happening when it's happening. It takes somebody like you to make me look back in retrospect, but I would say there was a rather monumental decision that somehow the Lord enabled me to make when I was very young and I don't know why I made this decision, and that was that when I came out of seminary, I decided that I was going to preach the Bible verse by verse, and mine out the theology because this was something that I didn't see happening. My dad did that toward the end of his ministry, in the early years he was more of an evangelist but toward the end he went through the book of Acts, the Gospel of John, the book of Romans, but there wasn't really any model for an in-depth theological exposition unless maybe it was David Martyn Lloyd-Jones, but he was in the text and then he was everywhere like Barnhouse was. But I just decided, my passion from the time I was a kid was to understand what the Bible meant by what it said. It wasn't so much the preaching, I wanted to know what this means by what it says. My heritage was to have absolute unwavering confidence in the Word of God. It was everything to me, absolutely everything to me, and I needed to cut it straight, I needed to get right.

> *I decided that I was going to preach the Bible verse by verse and mine out the theology because this was something that I didn't see happening.*

So when I went to seminary, it wasn't with a view of ministry; it was a view of getting the tools to rightly divide the Word of God and then I decided that I would explain the Bible with the Bible. If you've heard me preach, now that I've said that you understand that. I don't do a lot of current events. I don't talk about what's going on in the culture. I don't preach off the headlines in the newspaper.

I try to explain the Bible with the Bible because the Bible is its own best interpreter because it has one Author—it's what's called *Analogia Scripturae* in Latin. The Scripture is analogous to itself because it has a single Author. So the Bible is its own best interpreter and very young in my ministry I said I'm going to explain the Bible with the Bible and I'm going to stay out of the headlines, I'm going to stay out of the culture, I'm going to explain

the Bible the way the Bible is written from the Bible which keeps it in its context.

Little did I know at that time that the effect of that has been that the sermons I preached over these last fifty years don't have any cultural bounds on them. They are not dated. They are not tied to any current events, essentially they're not tied to anything happening in the culture. I'm not listening to the pundits. I'm not reading the newspapers. I'm explaining the Bible with the Bible and that's why it always amazes me, you know this from your years at Grace to You, I mean, there's what, 400,000 Vietnamese that listen to me every day because four people are translating everything I preach into Vietnamese and they are putting these little chips in little recorders and here they are in Vietnam hearing what I preached in southern California at Grace Community Church and it transcends all boundaries.

I just thought that was right to let the Word of God speak and to make sure that I didn't timestamp it with any kind of current cultural limitations.

The second thing was that once I began to preach expositionally, people would say, "We haven't heard this kind of an exposition. We haven't heard this," and they started sending tapes and those tapes started going around the world, and so the reason I started traveling was people around the world asked me to come and they would say, "Could you come and do a conference?" That's how it started wherever it was from South Africa to Asia and wherever, Russia or anywhere, they would say, "Could you come and do a conference and preach the Word of God like that?" And I would do that and I would do it again.

Once I began to preach expositionally, people would say, "We haven't heard this kind of an exposition. We haven't heard this," and they started sending tapes and those tapes started going around the world.

I was all over the place doing that and they would come back and say, "Now look, we want to learn how to do that. Can you come and teach us or can you come and we'll have a pastors' conference and we'll teach pastors how to do this?" Then the next wave was, "Okay, I can't be going everywhere all the time so can you send some guys from your church, some of your pastors including people like you, to come to our country and train pastors?"

And then it turned into, "Can we start a school here?" And that's why there are about thirty-five pastoral training centers now around the world all manned by graduates of Master's Seminary teaching the same thing there that we taught them at the Master's Seminary. So the only reason I went around the world was because they invited me to come and to teach the Word of God in a way that they wanted to learn how to do it, so we were able to kind of spread exposition around the globe. In those days, you had to go to do that. Now our guys are there and they are located all over the planet and they've learned the language and these schools are all in the native language, and every single one of them is at the invitation of the leaders of the local churches in those countries.

Don: Great encouragement to you, no doubt, to see that exponential multiplication of the ministry philosophy that's guided you from the start.

John: Yeah, and a typical illustration comes to mind. We had a guy who came to our seminary from Madagascar off the coast of Africa. This guy came out of nowhere with his wife and three kids, and that's not easy to come from Madagascar to southern California. What does he want? He wants to learn to handle the Word of God; he wants to go back to the church that he was in and they want him to be the pastor and he wants to start a training center. So he comes, and four years later, he's back home. He has taken two graduates and their families, and now there are three families back in Madagascar running a pastoral training center. That's a model for what happens.

> *There are probably fifty different cities now around the world that have asked us to come so we're trying to pump out enough graduates to meet that need in the future. And again, if you handle the Word correctly and you let the Bible speak, it's timeless and it's not bound by any culture.*

The same thing has happened in Lebanon. We have opened a pastoral training center in the Arabic language in Lebanon. That just keeps happening. There are probably fifty different cities now around the world that have asked us to come so we're trying to pump out enough graduates to meet that need in the future. And again, if you handle the Word correctly and you let the Bible speak, it's timeless and it's not bound by any culture. That's why people around the world download sermons because in any culture the Word of God is the Word of God.

Don: Your longevity in ministry has straddled different generations of preachers. You've fought battles alongside men like James Montgomery Boice and R. C. Sproul for the inerrancy of Scripture and against Roman Catholicism. Those men are now in heaven, but they were men of granite. They did not move.

Today, it seems to me like the environment is different. On September 4th, you published an article that appeared on the Social Justice website titled "No Division in the Body," and you were addressing the way that men that you've served alongside in this generation seem to be going after a different agenda. You said a line that was very poignant to me, "I thought we were together for the gospel," indicating, "Where did you guys go?" It seems like there is a difference on some issues compared to the shoulder-to-shoulder unwavering support that you had from men like Boice and R. C. Sproul. Give us some perspective on that. It seems like these are treacherous times. Point us in the right direction as we look at what's happening around us.

John: The original issue with Jim Boice was the inerrancy issue. He set up that Inerrancy Congress that ran for ten years, but there was another issue with Jim Boice that was deeply, deeply concerning to him and that was the Lordship issue, and most people don't know, they don't associate him with that but he wrote a book on discipleship that just nailed the issue of the Lordship of Christ...

Don: He wrote a foreword for *The Gospel According to Jesus*.

John: . . . and then that's why he wrote the foreword for *The Gospel According to Jesus*, and he came to Grace Church and he preached at Grace Church. In fact, my dad was there and he was so moved by that that he put a picture of Boice in his office on his desk so that he would remember to pray for him. But Boice was a champion for inerrancy and a champion for the Lordship of Christ, something that we assume is very basic but was under attack.

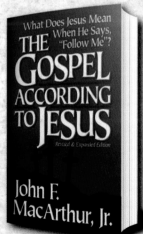

Sproul equally on those two doctrines, but Sproul, I mean, I was kind of an outsider because he was a Presbyterian and I was not and he was, you know, basically nurtured in the Reformed creedal kind of environment and I was just a student of the Bible. But he had the heart of a warrior like Boice did and you couldn't move him. He had a huge, huge heart of love and compassion. Sometimes you don't see that in strong, strong men.

I remember when he called me one day and he said, "I want to debate you on infant baptism," and I said, "R. C., you've got to be crazy. You don't have a prayer in that debate. There's not even one Bible verse you can lean on." And it was just his wonderful nature, he said, "No, I think it will really help people if we discuss it and I'm ready to do that." And he did that at a Ligonier conference and it's been a famous thing and that was the openness of his heart. But he used to call me Boris, that was his nickname because one time Boris Yeltsin, the Russian premier stood up on a tank and stopped the troops and he said, "That's MacArthur, he stands on the tank and stops whatever's coming. He stops the enemy, I want him in my foxhole," he would always say. Interestingly enough, last week I received a handwritten sweet note from Vesta, R. C.'s wife, thanking me on his behalf for the stand I took on social justice and telling me she was sad that he wasn't here to stand alongside of me.

> *"That's MacArthur, he stands on the tank and stops whatever's coming. He stops the enemy, I want him in my foxhole," [R.C. Sproul] would always say.*

There are warriors and I felt like the last man standing, you know, because all these guys are going and we're glad for young men like you and others that the Lord is raising up, but this is a generation that has decided to chase the culture and I'll tell you what happens: you start to chase the culture and you say, "Well, they don't like the old church music, they don't like exposition of the Scripture, they don't like serious worship, so we're going to adjust the style." And we've all seen that, they adjusted the style to reach the culture, and I've been saying going back to *Ashamed of the Gospel*, they're not going to be content with you adjusting the style. Do you understand what you're doing? That is the slippery slope. That's the downgrade controversy of Spurgeon, once you adjust the style, they've got you. The next thing they're going to do is make you adjust the message. So the social justice issue is a cultural message they are forcing on the church because the church has already said it's going to chase the world.

> *That's the downgrade controversy of Spurgeon, once you adjust the style, they've got you. The next thing they're going to do is make you adjust the message. So the social justice issue is a cultural message they are forcing on the church because the church has already said it's going to chase the world.*

Just as a comment on that, if there is one word that doesn't need an adjective it's "justice." That doesn't need an adjective. Justice is justice. So what they are talking about is not justice, they're talking about social issues but to try to make that part of the gospel and if you don't make it part of the gospel they're not going to accept you, this is a trap and they are all caught in the trap and they are not done. They are allowing the gospel if you add this, but pretty soon they won't want the gospel and they'll go exactly the way all the liberal churches went: first they wanted to adjust the style, then they wanted to accommodate the culture and keep the gospel, and eventually the culture wouldn't let them even keep the gospel and the gospel was gone.

Don: The gospel gets in the way of those agendas. That's the problem for them.

John: If you're going to take your cues from the world, they hate the gospel. They hate it and they're going to let you give them all the ground you want to give them and pretty soon you're going to wake up like the frog in the kettle and you've been fried.

Don: We're grateful, John, to be able to be here in a time when your presence in the broader body of Christ is still felt in support of the truth of Scripture, the truth of Christ, the truth of the gospel, and in a secondary horizontal sense, to have your voice joining with Boice and Sproul and other guys like that. It's a privilege to have you in our church for the second time in six months.

> ### *"Woe is me" if I preach not the gospel. I don't understand how anybody can do any other than preach the truth.*

John: Well, thank you and, you know, it is just "Woe is me" if I preach not the gospel. I don't understand how anybody can do any other than preach the truth. Whatever the climate, whatever the tolerances or intolerances are, I can honestly say I have never been shot at more than I'm being shot at now with false accusations, things that are not at all true, and the only thing that provides some measure of defense is that I'm so old and there is a track record of preaching the Word of God and ministry that sort of stands in the way of making all the accusations credible. But as I told you earlier, Don, I worry about young pastors who go out and try to take a stand, people take shots at them, they don't have any history to convince people that they are trustworthy. It's not going to be easy for them in the future.

Don: John, I know that people want to hear you preach and I need to get out of the way. Any final thoughts before you come to our pulpit?

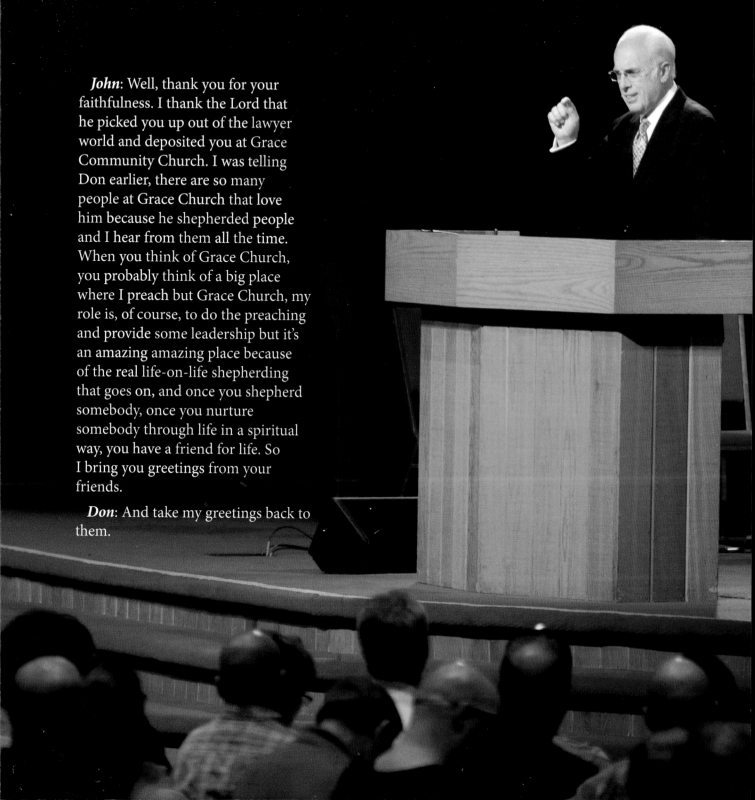

John: Well, thank you for your faithfulness. I thank the Lord that he picked you up out of the lawyer world and deposited you at Grace Community Church. I was telling Don earlier, there are so many people at Grace Church that love him because he shepherded people and I hear from them all the time. When you think of Grace Church, you probably think of a big place where I preach but Grace Church, my role is, of course, to do the preaching and provide some leadership but it's an amazing amazing place because of the real life-on-life shepherding that goes on, and once you shepherd somebody, once you nurture somebody through life in a spiritual way, you have a friend for life. So I bring you greetings from your friends.

Don: And take my greetings back to them.

For more details about John MacArthur and his Bible-teaching resources, contact Grace to You at 800-55-GRACE or gty.org.

To learn more about Don Green and his Bible-teaching resources, visit thetruthpulpit.com. You can subscribe to podcasts of his full-length messages from Truth Community Church, the daily "The Truth Pulpit" radio program, and his weekly feature "Through the Psalms." Also, be sure to look for Don's forthcoming book, *Trusting God in Trying Times* (Trust the Word Press, 2022).